THE RECRUITING BLUEPRINT

6 STEPS TO NAVIGATING YOUR RECRUITING PROCESS

APRIL PHILLIPS

Copyright © 2020 April Phillips, Hoop Haus LLC
All rights reserved. No part of this publication may reproduced, disturbed or transmitted in any form or by any means, including photocopy, recording, or other electronic or mechanical methods, without the prior written permission of the author, except in the case of brief quotations embodied in critical reviews and certain other noncommercial uses permitted by copyright law. For permission request, contact the author.
April.Phillips@hoophaus.com

ISBN: 978-1-7357821-02

THE RECRUITING BLUEPRINT:
Six Steps To Navigating Your Recruiting Process

Written by

APRIL PHILLIPS

Shop Hoop Haus
Use Code
THEBLUEPRINT
FOR 20% OFF

DEDICATION

To every little black girl with a dream. You are strong, you are valued, you are appreciated. Go out into the world and be unapogetically, a savage.

To Anne Donovan, who lead with purpose and character. Thank you for seeing something in me and pulling me into the profession. Thank you for teaching me that people come first. Rest in heaven, "My Anne."

Contents

Dedictation I
Contents II
Acknowledgments VII
Introduction IX
    Coaching Changes XI
    Instant Gratification XII
    The Recruiting Process XII

Chapter 1: Be Recruitable 1
    Academics 2
    NCAA Requirements 2
    Be Good Enough 5
    Activity 1.1 | ATHLETIC SKILL ASSESSMENT 6

Chapter 2: CHARACTER & LOYALTY MATTERS 9
    Relationships 11
    On the Court 14
    Activity 2.1 | NEGATIVE CHARACTERISTICS 15
        Being a Bad Teammate 15
        Bad Body Language 15
        Being Un-Coachable 15
    Activity 2.2 | POSITIVE CHARACTERISTICS 16
        Being a Good Teammate 16
        Good Body Language 16
        Being Coachable 16
    Off The Court 18

- Activity 2.3 | SOCIAL MEDIA DON'TS 22
  - Basketball 22
  - Dating 22
  - General Topics 22
- Activity 2.4 | SOCIAL MEDIA DO'S 23
  - Basketball 23
  - Dating 23
  - General Topics 23

Chapter 3: PARENTS, YOU MATTER TOO 26
- Coach bashing 27
- Sideline coach 28
- Coach harasser 29

Chapter 4: How do I get Noticed? 31
- Have a Recruiting Package 31
- Transcripts and Test Scores 32
- Highlight and Game Film 32
- Create a Realistic Target List 33
- Recruit The Target 35

Chapter 5: Respect the Process 38
- Narrow Your Focus 38
- Be Realistic 40
- Go On Unofficial Visits 43
- Narrow your focus 44
- Relationship building 45
- Communicate 45

Chapter 6: THE DECISION 47

    What's Important to You? 48

    Determine your non-negotiables 48

    Activity 6.1| NON-NEGOTIABLES 49

    Activity 6.2 | OFFERS 50

    Elimination 50

    Activity 6.3 | PROS & CONS 53

    Activity 6.4 | EVALUATION 58

    Activity 6.5 | COMPARING 60

My unsolicited two cents 61

A LETTER FROM THE AUTHOR 65

Tools & Resources 67

Websites 69

Questions to Ask College Coaches 71

About Hoop Haus 73

About The Author 75

ACKNOWLEDGMENTS

I have been working on this book for a number of years. It has felt as though I continued to just allow it to fall on the back burner. Through the years, I received an immense amount of support and push from my brother, Patrick, my mother Robbie, and a handful of close friends. While I do not have a coauthor for this project, it is important that I acknowledge the coaches who have mentored me over the years as well as those who I have had the pleasure of working with. I thank the late, great, Anne Donovan, Ty Grace, Bonnie Hendrickson, Katrina Merriweather, and Torino Johnson. I also thank Charity Elliott who gave me my first division 1 opportunity as a coach and recruiting coordinator. You all were and are a part of my journey, and I thank you.

To all of the student athletes and parents that I have had the pleasure of getting to know through recruiting, I thank you for growing me, making me better and helping me to develop my own personal philosophy on recruiting.

INTRODUCTION

Being recruited by colleges is an exciting experience. For most, it's a huge milestone en route to the ultimate goal: receiving a full athletic scholarship to an institution where you will continue your academic and athletic career. It feels good to be wanted, to be recognized for the hard work you've put into the game, and, ultimately, to be on the verge of accomplishing something that not many are afforded the opportunity to do. Make no mistake, this is a big deal that's often taken for granted. Don't be that person.

I recall getting my first letter in the mail and the tremendous excitement I felt. To this day, I have a box that contains all of my letters from when I was in high school. I thank my mother for that. There is zero probability that I would have saved them all this time. I still remember my first letter and the first coach who reached out to me. That moment is something to remember. However, what I know now—and you may know it by now, too—is that, as you get older and venture further into the recruiting process, it's not the letter that matters, but the regular communication and the offer. (Note: DO NOT belittle regular communication if an offer has yet to be extended. More on this later). But, to eighth-grade April, that first letter from, from a PAC-10 institution, was everything. As the kids would say nowadays, I was lit! It meant that I was noticed and that I had a shot at being a collegiate athlete. Enjoy that moment when it comes. It's special. The landscape of recruiting has changed dramatically over the years, and ideas and philosophies on how the recruiting process should work vary widely. Whether you're a college or club coach, scouting service, player, parent, step-dad, family pet ... everyone has an opinion and those opinions often differ from one another considerably.

As a college basketball coach, I am often tasked with one of the most important aspects of a college basketball program: recruiting. I spend countless hours on the phone, in the gym, etc., doing the best job I can for my institution, and also for the student athletes I come into contact with. I pride myself on the fact that my relationships are real, and while of course I want what's good for my program, I also want what's best for the young women and families I work with and get to know very well. I see young ladies make great decisions, but I also see some not-so-great ones. It's part of the game. As the transfer topic becomes more and more relevant, I want more young athletes to feel that they've gutted through the recruiting process thoroughly and feel like they know what they're doing. Whatever comes after that is what shall be and is meant to be. However, if I can succeed in helping a few student athletes navigate the process a bit more efficiently, my heart will be full and my mission accomplished.

As a college athlete, I transferred. Back then, there was no online portal, just a release form and a fax machine. Imagine faxing your release to every school you're interested in! That's what the transfer process was like for me. As a freshman, I attended Georgia Institute of Technology (GT) and would later have a semester-long stint at Florida A&M, prior to finding what I believe was my ultimate best fit: Xavier University in Cincinnati.

Recently, our game has seen a spike in transfer numbers at the college level. Everyone has a theory as to what's driving the increase. Among the reasons you'll hear are, it's the college coaches selling false dreams; it's the student athletes thinking they're better than they are; it's the student athletes not willing to be patient; it's the parents pushing their kids to go too high; it's the college coaches who don't have relationships with their team—the list goes on. I can't claim to know for sure why the numbers spike, but I do have a few ideas:

> **1. COACHING CHANGES** – This is a factor that we know exists. A head coach leaves, and then a player wants to leave given that the new situation will not be the same with the new head coach. I get it, and so do most people. It's like getting a

new boss who you don't quite click with in the same way, or a new landlord who wants to change your lease terms. Time to move on! Some people think, well, you sign with the school, not the coach, and it's true. Sort of. Let's just say that every situation is different and leave it at that.

2. INSTANT GRATIFICATION – We live in a world in which everything is at our fingertips. We want it now! The respect and admiration for the process of achieving amazing things simply doesn't exist anymore. "I deserve it, and I want it now." "I was ranked number 20 in high school, and so I should play right now, as freshman. I shouldn't have to wait." Yes, there are scenarios in which a potential student athlete (PSA) may come in as a freshman and start. And then there are scenarios where a PSA might not get much playing time in her freshman year and then go on to become a starter and all-conference player her junior and senior years. Again, every situation is different, and I have no strong opinion.

3. THE RECRUITING PROCESS – This is the reason you opened this book, right? How our student athletes come to their decisions needs to be addressed. The process has to be taken more seriously and vetted more thoroughly. Too many student PSAs don't ask the right questions or do adequate research, or they make decisions based on personal priorities.

My experience as a student athlete is the reason why I hold recruiting so close to my heart. It's why I attempt to recruit in a way that I believe is the right way. I simply want to see more student athletes make the right choices the first time around. Your college choice influences your life journey massively. These decisions must be made without distraction and be in sync with your priorities.

With the rapid growth of AAU basketball, ranking platforms, recruiting services, Instagram pages, and tweets, it's easy to forget that you are indeed a small piece of the big picture. The opportunity to have coaches recruit you to join their rosters should not be taken for granted. Whether junior college, D3, NAIA, D2, mid-major, or BCS, don't underestimate the privilege of being a student athlete to whom coaches reach out. The most important thing in this entire process is finding your best fit, regardless of level. Your situation is unique, and your fit differs from everyone else's fit, including your teammate, best friend, sister, whomever ... and that's OK. You want to be able to look back on your college journey once you're done and be in love with your experience ... well, maybe not every moment, but overall, with the experience and the process. The process is bigger than basketball; it's a total person evaluation.

While you're obviously in this situation because you're a basketball player, there are other aspects of becoming a college athlete that you must not overlook or fail to evaluate. How does your degree from this institution fit with your life goals? How will the program promote your future career? What's the mental health support like? Are the school's past student athletes happy with their experience? Is the program transactional or transformative? What are your opportunities in the area after college?

These are some of the things that we'll discuss regarding the decision process, but you will also get some nuggets to help you navigate the process along the way, which ultimately, hopefully, ends with you finding your best fit.

What I like to call the "bells and whistles" of the recruiting process is an amazing experience, a once-in-a-lifetime event for you, provided that you don't go for round two out of the portal. Remember, it's a daily routine for college coaches like myself. At the end of the day, college basketball is a business. Some operate in it with more care than others, but it is a business, and every college coach has a job to do. A big part of that job is to sign players they believe will help their program succeed. A variety of core values exist among coaches, and many have their own ideas as to what success in their program looks like, but please don't be fooled; there's a job to be done. Hence, when you're being recruited by an institution, it's because the staff sees you as someone who can potentially help them get that job done.

I've tried to be transparent in writing this book. Based on the knowledge I have gained from being on the other side, this is the advice I would give my own daughter, sister, cousin, or family friend. The "coaches hive" could very well be after me following this, but you can rest assured that my intention with this book is to benefit student athletes, parents, AAU coaches—everyone hoping to assist a PSA in making the best of her once-in-a-lifetime college recruiting process. Although on most days I'm a college basketball coach, for this book I'm putting myself on your side of the fence.

§

My goal is to not only share with you some pertinent information, but also identify the things you may already know subconsciously but haven't focused on. All in all, these words are designed to assist you in your quest to compete at the next level and get through the recruiting process. Whether you have yet to begin the process and are unsure of the proper steps to follow, or already have offers in hand and aren't sure how to narrow your choices, the information I'll share with you will meet you where you are in the process and help you find your best-fit program.

As a reminder, this text represents the opinions of just one person, and there are many others. It's not the recruiting Bible, much less some kind of crystal ball. My hope is that you'll take a couple of useful nuggets with you, snippets that stand out and resonate, and that help you in your process. I'm not here to tell you what's the "right way" or the "wrong way." There's no such thing. Your job is to take the bits of advice that resonate with you and leave the rest. This book is for *YOU*, and I hope it's informative and helpful. I also encourage you to visit HoopHaus.com for my Hoop Haus Chronicles blogs for more thoughts on the recruiting process.

Questions for Colleges
- What is the academic requirement to play at this college?

1
BE RECRUITABLE

Don't just be wanted. Be desirable. Have the grades or have a seat.

Playing professional basketball is an awesome opportunity that not many are granted. Always keep in mind, though, that the opportunity doesn't last forever. Your education matters. The odds of becoming a professional women's basketball player are slim. Think of it as a pyramid, as depicted in the image shown here. The truth is that there are fewer opportunities in women's pro basketball than in the men's game. I'm not trying to discourage you, but rather to give you a realistic perspective.

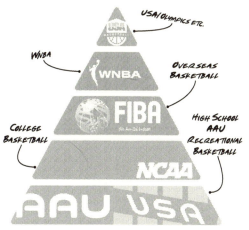

Harsh truths are no less true than happy ones. I don't know about your particular talent level or work ethic. You could very well go on to become a professional athlete, and I encourage you to pursue that goal. If you have the work ethic and the talent, you could make it to the top of the game. You know you better than I do. As they say, shoot for the stars and you might just land among them. Just know that a handful of PSAs have the opportunity to further their careers at the professional level. What does being recruitable mean?" Having the grades and being good enough. Let's dive in!

Academics

The NCAA has a set of academic standards for the various levels of college basketball. If these standards mean nothing else to you, know that being a great basketball player is not more important than your education. To begin with, if you don't have the grades, you will not play, period. If you haven't done your work in the classroom and scored well on the standardized test, you won't be signing on that dotted line come signing day. There are various routes you can take, and the standards are different for each level, but standards do exist.

Beyond needing adequate grades to participate in the sport, you'll also need solid academics to prepare for life after the sport. Getting signed and playing might seem like everything now, but your education will serve you well for the rest of your life if you give it the same level of dedication and effort you do to playing. It's something no one can take from you, so take it seriously.

NCAA Requirements

There's life after basketball. If you haven't taken this statement to heart, you definitely should. In fact, the NCAA has made significant efforts to ensure that you do. If you don't show proper dedication to your academics, you can lose your right to be a college athlete. The NCAA has put into place qualifications that PSAs must attain prior to accepting a college scholarship and signing a national letter of intent. This bears repeating: You will not be allowed to play at the college level if you do not fit the requirements set forth by the NCAA for your division and level.

NCAA qualifications change from time to time, and so I will not attempt to summarize them here. Be sure to spend some time at the NCAA website reviewing the latest information. Know what's required early! Don't wait until your junior year of high school to start thinking about eligibility. If you're truly engrossed in the game, you'll know whether you want to play college ball. Be prepared! Start before you begin your freshman year of high school. Know which courses you need to take and what requirements they satisfy.

As you look at the requirements, you'll notice that they're more stringent at the division-one level. It's safe to say that if you use the division one scale as your model, you'll be NCAA qualifiable at the division 2, 3, etc. levels (please note that I said NCAA "qualifiable." Individual academic institutions have their own requirements for admission, which we will not cover here).

NCAA requirements for playing college basketball can get a little complicated. You need to make sure you understand the requirements for grades and standardized test scores. You can do this by researching the NCAA Eligibility Center (contact information can be found on our Important Resources page), and talking to your guidance counselor, AAU coach, and/or college basketball coaches. It's important to build relationships with counselors, teachers etc. because they're important resources. Be the kid they want to recommend! Keep in mind, though, that counselors, AAU coaches, and even high school coaches don't always know the NCAA requirements for student athletes. Perhaps they don't have any prior experience with student athletes with your potential. The point is, don't stop there. Seek out the information you need. Own your journey.

If you're being recruited, most coaches won't mind running an evaluation on your academic standing and helping you understand the requirements and what's expected of you. For most, if not all schools, if they're recruiting you, they'll want to run the evaluation. Note: Always have your most recent transcript available as a PDF file or a scanned image of the original. Be prepared! Many schools won't accept screen shots. You need a document that includes your full name, school name, etc.

Be in the know, and make use of the resources and people who know things that can help you. The Internet is your friend! Take some time to research the things that will affect your future. You've probably heard coaches tell you to "control the controllable," and that includes your course enrollment and transcripts. Don't miss out on opportunities come junior and senior year because you didn't understand the requirements. You'd be surprised how often schools want to make an offer to a PSA, but can't because that PSA is a questionable qualifier. Don't let your transcripts hurt your chances. They should scream, "I got my stuff together!"

One more thing: If you're in close consideration for a late offer, your transcripts can definitely tip the scales in your favor. Give yourself every possible advantage to receive more opportunities.

Be Good Enough

Your game is obviously an important part of the whole recruiting process. Improving over time is important. We live in a world of social media. I'm actually quite fond of social media (give your girl a follow, by the way!), and I recognize that it can be a double-edged sword. Don't be the hyped kid who doesn't produce. Don't be the one with Instagram and twitter highlight pages proclaiming you as one of the top kids in your class in eighth grade and then never get better. How many times have we seen a young phenom with nearly the same game four years later? Even though social media has become a major part of recruiting, don't forget that your game is an even bigger part. Work on it. There's more to basketball than crossovers and highlight reels. Take the time to evaluate your game. What are you good at? What could you improve? What separates you from the crowd? Complete activity 1.1 below. Take the time to assess your game. Be brutally honest with yourself about your strengths, as well as those that need improvement. It's the only way to move forward.

ACTIVITY 1.1
ATHLETIC SKILL ASSESSMENT | In this assessment write your skills in the skill column and rate that skill in the rating column (below average, average, above average and elite)

SKILL	RATING
Mid-range shooting	Below Avg
ball handling	Elite
shooting	above average
defense	~~above~~ average
IQ	above average
ball handling	average
Mid-range	above average
3-point	elite
passing	above average
post-work	below average

Now that you've assessed your strong points, you'll want to continue to work to improve them. This way, you'll become the most elite version of yourself possible in the areas that come most naturally to you. For the areas that aren't your strong suits, work on them until they don't stick out like a sore thumb. Will you ever be just as good in your weaker areas as you are in your strong ones? Maybe not, but at least you'll be competent at them to the point that they don't stand out as weaknesses. For example, if your evaluation says that one of your strong points is rim drives right and one of your weakest points is rim drives left, continue to add on the options you have for rim drives right. Add to your finishing packet—ways that you're capable of finishing at the rim (e.g., reverse lay-up, euro step, rondo, spin, etc.). As for that left hand, concentrate on being efficient getting there. A left-hand drive doesn't have to be your go-to, but is it an option when defense forces you to it? Can you make a play to that left hand if it's the best play in the moment, or will you force a play to your right hand? You need to be able to make the play.

In addition to getting into the gym regularly to work on your skills, watch the game. If you want to be a college ball player, watch college ball. Pretty simple. The same goes for watching WNBA games. Don't obsess over the NBA and neglect the WNBA. These are women who've been where you want to go. They deserve your respect. I'm not saying you shouldn't watch the NBA, but let's give our WNBA players a little love as well. When someone asks a young female athlete who their favorite player is, let's throw some WNBA players' names into the mix. Our game / craft isn't going to grow unless we get out there and grow it. Plus, doing so benefits you!

2
CHARACTER & LOYALTY MATTERS

Coaches watch your mannerisms on and off the court.
They're recruiting the total you, not just the athlete you.
Who you are can turn coaches on or off.

You're about to read the longest chapter in this book, and it's that way for a reason. The things discussed in these pages are becoming highlighted more and more in the recruiting process. Take notes.

College coaches are looking for a total package. Your athletic ability is the initial eye-catcher that will spark interest in you as a potential student-athlete at their institution; however, once you've drawn their interest in your game, you've also invited their interest in every other aspect of your life. They want to know who you are, not just how well you play. Think about it; there are probably hundreds, perhaps even thousands, of girls with nearly identical skill sets. They dribble just as well as you do, pass just as well, shoot just as well, and defend just as well, too. What separates you from them?

To be very clear, I'm not denying that there are extremely elite players, whose talents are unmatched or that compare to a very small, very elite group of players. If you're one of those players, you still need to separate yourself from your peers. Yes, this elite group is a much smaller one, so as a high-level elite athlete, you may have some wiggle room. Right, wrong, or indifferent, staffs will weigh the pros and cons of an elite player with some "baggage." By this, I mean elements that are not necessarily ideal when that particular staff looks at the total package for their institution. Keep in mind, this can and does vary from school-to-school, and staff-to-staff.

Throughout your process, I want you to take interest in controlling what you can control. In my opinion, there are two factors that go into recruiting that you, the PSA, have absolutely no control over: geography and existing relationships. Geography may be one factor that separates you from the nationwide pool of young women with essentially the same skills. You may just happen to be local to a particular institution. This means that the school would be able to see you more, they'll get to know you and your game, and you can visit the campus unofficially more often and build relationships. The staff may feel that they have a better shot at recruiting you to join their program than they do someone from outside the area. Many college basketball staffs like the idea of taking care of home … if you fit what they're looking for.

On the other hand, being local can be a disadvantage. I have a theory that a local school might possibly see you too much and perhaps start to appreciate less what you bring to the table or see your flaws more, whereas being "wowed" by someone they see four times a year across the country at July events could leave them more excited. Take it for what it is: a theory. My theory.

RELATIONSHIPS

Relationships are another factor that you have no control over. The recruiting coach may have a relationship with your HS or AAU coach or otherwise affiliated persons. This usually means there's trust between the programs, which means that the college coach will trust your HS or AAU coach not to oversell you and can vouch for your skill level and ability to compete at that college's level. It could also be the college coach trusting your HS coach, AAU coach or other affiliate to vouch for your character, work ethic, and family, or make an all-around evaluation as to whether a particular program might be a good fit for you.

Another aspect of the relationship factor that you have no control over could be that a college coach feels they might get a fair shot at a PSA from a particular program where there's familiarity. For example, I'm looking at Ashley and Ariel. Ashley plays for ABC club and Ariel plays for XYZ club. Both Ashley and Ariel have very similar games, and either of them would fit our need for the upcoming signing class. As it turns out, I've known the coach of ABC club for 10 years, but I don't know the coach of XYZ club very well. Can you guess which player I'm going to recruit harder? I know that, because of my relationship with the coach of ABC club, I can call and get honest information, and I'm going to trust that coach to share what they know of me and the program. If I can't get a hold of the player, I can trust that this coach will assist me.

In a situation like this, the coach of ABC club isn't going to push that PSA my way, but there's a level of comfort and trust there, and it makes a difference. Will I still recruit Ariel? Yes, of course. A good college coach should always work on building trusting relationships with club or AAU coaches. I just want to you to know that this relationship factor is something over which you have no control in your recruiting process. These types of relationships in the recruiting world can give you an added boost, or they can put you at a slight disadvantage. So, although Ashley has a slight edge at my school, Ariel is going to have that same advantage at another school. There's enough to go around.

In addition to the uncontrollable factors that go into recruiting, there are controllable factors, too, which are totally in your hands. These are the small things that can easily put college coaches off of you or on to you. Coaches understand that you're young, and you still have maturing to do. No one expects perfection, but ask yourself the following question: "Are there flaws in my character, attitude, effort, or loyalty?" These are things that are controllable and correctable if they exist, but that can also be seen as "headaches" or "baggage," as mentioned earlier.

Always be looking to expand your opportunities. You don't want to have roadblocks or red flags, not if you can control it, anyway. These things can put a question mark over your head when it comes to finding the right fit for team chemistry or coachability. Showcasing questionable traits in the areas of character, attitude, effort, and loyalty might leave staffs having to decide if your positives outweigh any negative character, attitude, effort, or loyalty issues. These areas turn the focus away from your physical talents and toward your manageability if you were to join their program. Will you do things that don't align with the core values of the program? On the other hand, there are times when strong character, a good attitude, extreme effort, and loyalty can increase a recruit's desirability. Then the conversation turns to, "she'll be good for our culture, and she'll fit in well with our team."

Honestly, these elements may affect you differently based on a program's level of interest in you or the level of player you are. It's just a fact. I'm not here to lie to you. If you have 30 offers, these things may affect you less than they would a player with 3 offers, as it relates directly to your recruiting process. I'm not encouraging you not to worry about your baggage as long as you have plenty of offers. You should want to be an outstanding teammate and person anyway. Duh! Is it fair? No, but right, wrong, or indifferent, it all boils down to a simple risk/benefit evaluation. That's it. Look at it this way: Let's say it's rumored that you steal from your teammates, you're difficult to get along with, and you jump from club to club every summer. Is there another kid, one who has no issues with character, attitude, effort, or loyalty who may have an equally or slightly less developed skill set than you? If so, a staff may take more of a liking to, and put more effort into, that kid and trust their ability to develop them a bit to make up for their deficits. That young lady may get the offer, while you get the letters.

Next, let's explore on-the-court and off-the-court red and green flags for college coaches.

On The Court

Coaches are going to take notice of your on-court mannerisms, how you communicate with your teammates, how you take coaching, how long it takes you to run down the floor after you believe you got fouled and yet no whistle was blown, how you come to the bench after the coach pulls you following a turnover, how you respond when you make a million-dollar pass and your teammate misses the lay up … these are all areas that you have the power to control and should be alerted to.

During evaluation periods, coaches are there, sitting on the sidelines, with their books in hand. There are times that they know who they're looking at, and although they're there to evaluate that one player, if you're on the court, you have an opportunity to be noticed as well.

Regardless of whether it's you they came to see or someone else, how will you stand out, positively, or negatively? Will you get a circle around your name, or a line through it? Before moving on, let's see what things you believe could be characterized as being negative or positive in the various categories by completing activities 2.1 and 2.2

ACTIVITY 2.1
NEGATIVE CHARACTERISTICS ASSESSMENT | In this assessment you will identify four behaviors that are considered or seen as negative in the following categories.

BEING A BAD TEAMMATE
1. _____
2. _____
3. _____
4. _____

BAD BODY LANGUAGE
1. _____
2. _____
3. _____
4. _____

BEING UN-COACHABLE
1. _____
2. _____
3. _____
4. _____

Activity 2.2

POSITIVE CHARACTERISTICS ASSESSMENT | In this assessment you will identify four behaviors that are considered or seen as positive in the following categories.

BEING A GOOD TEAMMATE
1. _____
2. _____
3. _____
4. _____

GOOD BODY LANGUAGE
1. _____
2. _____
3. _____
4. _____

BEING COACHABLE
1. _____
2. _____
3. _____
4. _____

We won't go into depth on the items you listed; this exercise is simply to help you be aware of your positives and negatives. For your reference, here are some items you may have filled in your sheet with. These items are controllable, and I encourage you to be more aware of your projections when you're on the court.

Negative Attitude

Being a Bad Teammate
- Complaining when a teammate makes a mistake
- Not acknowledging a teammate's encouragement
- Not slapping hands when a teammate reaches out to you
- Sitting on the bench mad and not supporting your team because you aren't in the game

Bad Body Language
- Making faces or hand gestures when a ref makes a call you don't agree with
- Holding your head down after a mistake
- Looks of lack of engagement/blank stares

Being Un/Coachable
- Insisting on explaining to your coach why you were right every time he or she attempts to correct you
- Not making eye contact when your coach is talking
- Not acknowledging that you hear or understand what your coach is saying

Positive Attitude

Being a Good Teammate
- Telling your teammate, "you got the next one" when they make a mistake
- Responding to positive interaction with teammates, e.g., a head nod, or a simple, "I got you," when your teammate is attempting to encourage you
- Cheering/encouraging your team on from the bench, even when you may not be having your best game
- Taking ownership for mistakes even when it's not your fault

Positive Body Language
- Accept ref's call and move on to huddling with your team, sprinting down the floor, etc.

- Play the next play: you miss a shot, turn the ball over, etc., have short-term memory and quickly direct your attention to the next play ... sprint back on defense, etc.
- Be engaged. Give off positive energy. This varies from person to person (e.g., clapping, smiling, head nods, slapping teammates' hands when walking by, old-school pat on the butt of a teammate).

Positive energy doesn't have to be vocal.

Be Coachable

- You listen and you are open to feedback
- Able to receive constructive criticism and correction
- Not taking correction personally
- Willing to look at your own performance to improve

Off The Court

Coaches want to know about you as a person. They want to know if you'll represent the program in a positive manner at all times. We see it all the time: off-court mishaps that not only reflect on the student athlete, but also the program and the institution. Think of it as a parent/child relationship. Everything you do while you're a minor under your parents' supervision reflects not only on you, but also on your parents. Your parents must answer for your actions. It's the same between student athlete and the college basketball program. The person you are matters.

As a student athlete, you're given the privilege to represent not only your team, but also the overall university. For many universities, athletic programs are important marketing tools. Fair or not, you'll be held to a higher standard than the general student body. If you get a DUI, you can be sure that it will make the papers, though one of your classmates who doesn't play sports might not get the same level of attention for a similar infraction. You know what they say, "to whom much is given, much is required." Well, in this case it's true.

Coaches will ask those who know you about your character. They'll ask not only your coaches, but also other coaches in your area. They'll ask the high school athletic director, and they'll ask your teammates—some of whom they may also be recruiting—how they like playing with you. The people around you are your walking resume. Let your everyday life make it a good one. Don't be fake, but do the right thing.

Your high school or AAU coaches are not going to lie for you, not the good ones, anyway. They can't say you're an amazing and highly coachable athlete if you aren't. Why? Remember what we said about relationships? If they lie for you, they're damaging their relationships with coaches and their reputations. This will interfere with opportunities for players that come from your program or school in the future, or any other players this coach talks about in the recruiting process. You're not the only or last player that your coach will want to help make it to the next level. If you remember just one thing, remember that character cannot be faked when college coaches are on the baseline. Your reputation, your character, is created every single day, with every single person you come in contact with. Always hold yourself to a high standard. Character is a huge part of recruiting, bigger than you know. Seriously, though, be good and do good for you. Do the right thing. Be a good person.

Don't get me wrong. I'm not suggesting that you live a little perfect life. It's impossible. We all make mistakes. College coaches, as some may forget, were all in high school once upon a time. We've all had lapses in judgment. Growth is necessary for everyone. In no way am I throwing a brick from a glass house. There's a difference between having an altercation at school and being known around campus as the girl not to be played with because you have had five fights since school began and it's only January. There is a difference between ditching once and never showing up for class. You get my drift, right? Rule of thumb: try to do good and be good. You owe that to you, if no one else.

Social Media

- Your social media activities reflect of you.
- Once you hit send, you cannot get it back
- There are different levels of sensitivity to social media content for sure.
- Do's and don'ts of social media
- Know when social media has gone too far.

Social media is huge these days, and it plays a huge part in this off-the-court piece. Your social media activities are a reflection of you. We live in a technological world where we have audiences of thousands, which, with a simple retweet, screenshot, share, or repost, could become hundreds of thousands. Once you hit send, you can't get it back. Even if you post something for just a few minutes before having a change of heart and taking it back down, your post could be captured by a screenshot. Once it's out there, it's out there. Be cautious, and don't be an impulsive tweeter, especially as it relates to your family, team, teammates, and coaches. This may be tough. We all know that once those fingers get moving, it's hard to stop them, because, honey, you have things to say! I know it, I feel you. But let me tell you something, drafts are a lifesaver.

There are different levels of sensitivity to social media content for sure. Some coaches, evaluators, or onlookers may have varying tolerances for what PSAs post, based on their backgrounds and beliefs. Again, no one is asking you to be perfect, just mindful. What's considered appropriate varies from person-to-person. There's no golden rule. A good rule-of-thumb might be that if your mom or dad wouldn't approve, then it probably shouldn't be on your page. Once you've decided your level of appropriate, just as with anything else, understand this: some people will accept you for you, and others will not. Just remember, you're not for everybody and not everybody is for you. Just be OK with owning your social media feed, good, bad, or indifferent.

Let's move on to a useful activity to test your ability to know when social media has gone too far. This will help you gauge your level of "appropriate." Reminder: this differs for everyone. Complete activities 2.3 and 2.4.

ACTIVITY 2.3

SOCIAL MEDIA DON'TS | Provide four statements that could be considered or seen as going too far for social media regarding the following topics. (Let's not get carried away here now) :

BASKETBALL

1. _____
2. _____
3. _____
4. _____

DATING

1. _____
2. _____
3. _____
4. _____

GENERAL TOPICS
(CELEBRITIES, SONGS, ENTERTAINMENT, ETC.)

1. _____
2. _____
3. _____
4. _____

Activity 2.4

SOCIAL MEDIA DO'S | Using the same examples from above (Activitity 2.3) and correct the examples so they are acceptable (A way that is fit for social media):

BASKETBALL

1. _____
2. _____
3. _____
4. _____

DATING

1. _____
2. _____
3. _____
4. _____

GENERAL TOPICS
(CELEBRITIES, SONGS, ENTERTAINMENT, ETC.)

1. _____
2. _____
3. _____
4. _____

Now that you've completed the exercises, let's talk about some of the things you may have made mention of in the "don'ts" category:

DON'TS

Basketball
- After a loss: rants about your coach

- Sub tweets that are clearly about a teammate not passing the ball or similar
- Anything that sheds negative light on your team or program

Dating
- After breaking up with an ex: full rant, revealing every negative thing about this person you can think of
- Videos of you making out with your partner—no one wants to see that—boyfriend, girlfriend, elephant, whatever

General
- Foul language
- Foul gifs/videos
- Nudity

In the same way that you need to be mindful of the content that you yourself put out there, you'll also want to be mindful of the things you retweet and "like." Social media tells your followers what you like and of course what you retweet and repost. Be sure to apply your own standards to others' content as well.

- Just because you didn't write it doesn't mean it's not a reflection on you. Likes and retweets show up as associated with your account. Even if you agree, sometimes it's best to just read it and move on.
- If you wouldn't write it, don't retweet it or like it.

Hopefully, this gives you a basis for developing your own standards. If you can't help yourself when posting, at least make yourself a "finsta" account and don't allow coaches and other recruiting influencers to follow you. Yes, I know about "finstas." We all do. But even on those, remember, the Internet is forever and everyone that follows you is not your friend. This may seem like a lot, overwhelming even. I repeat, no one expects you to be perfect. I know exactly what I did and thought when I was in high school. Most college staffs talk about growth being a process, and it doesn't happen all at once just from stepping onto campus. We understand the demographic we're dealing with. You should also know that the "uptight" type of coach will not see your content the same way as the "chill" type of coach will. You need to be OK with how and what you post affects your recruitment. Own it.

As much as I like to consider myself the chill type of coach, I've dropped PSAs after viewing their social media content. The common theme is the key word, "consistent." It's never been based on one tweet or one post. Rather, it's a pattern of tweets or posts that are lewd, profane, or what I deem as toxic to team culture. Personally, I love to see youth be youth, and because I continue to meet my recruits and players where they are, I enjoy learning about them, their generation, and their thought processes. I like to consider myself "down"! However, I'm not for everybody, and neither are you. Be OK with that. Your authentic self matters, in the recruiting process as in life. It's the only way to find a true fit. Just make sure you're not turning off the people, coaches, or schools you want to keep around. You want to be tactful and tasteful, not fake. There's a difference.

3
PARENTS, YOU MATTER TOO

Coaches are no longer recruiting just the student-athlete. They're recruiting the package, which, fortunately or unfortunately, includes you.

Mom, Dad, this chapter is for you! First, I want to commend you for opening this book because it means you're invested in your child's recruiting process. You understand the importance to your child of this process and this decision. From college coaches across the globe, I want to say thank you for the time, money, and sacrifices you invest in your child's basketball career. You are valued, and you are a super parent!

OK, Mom and Dad, on to the tough stuff: you count! You may not be able to get your child a scholarship, but you can surely lose one for them. Parents are more relevant now than ever before in the recruiting process. When your child becomes part of a team, the coach/staff/program also welcomes you into the family. Coaches are no longer just recruiting a student-athlete. They're recruiting an entire package, which, for better or worse, includes you. Different coaches have different levels of what that "welcome" may look like, but you are nonetheless a part of the four-year deal and beyond. Coaches consider the way you behave and communicate as something that will become a part of their program. In today's landscape of possible lawsuits, claims of verbal abuse and other mistreatment, parents/players addressing issues with administration etc., your temperament and how you handle situations and communication regarding and with your child really matter.

> "COACHES ARE NO LONGER SIMPLY RECRUITING A STUDENT-ATHLETE. THEY ARE NOW RECRUITING AN ENTIRE PACKAGE, WHICH, FOR BETTER OR WORSE INCLUDES YOU."

Let me be very clear and share with you some things that may turn off college coaches when dealing with parents. Mom, Dad, I preface this by saying that everyone's opinion and level of tolerance is different. You, too, are not for everybody. I implore you to find a balance that works for you. However, you do need to be aware of some of the types of things that college coaches take notice of and talk to each other about.

COACH BASHING

Bashing your child's high school coach to college coaches will not help your child. You're simply showing that college coach that you will feel no hesitation in bashing them and/or their program as well, should things not happen the way you want them to. There are scenarios in which of course we can see clear as day that the things you're saying may be true. Depending on the depth of your relationship with a given college coach, this can come off as a character trait notice, or simply conversation. In general, be careful about having those types of discussions and who you have them with, and err on the side of less criticism.

Sideline coach

Are you the parent in the stands who yells at the refs? Coaches your child during play? "Shoot the ball!" "Don't pass it to her, she won't pass it to you!" During timeouts, are your child's eyes in the huddles or in the stands? Do you yell at your child's teammates? "Pass the ball!" If this describes you, coaches will assume that you'll exhibit this behavior at their games, too. Now don't get me wrong; there are levels to this, and I'm not saying that parents shouldn't cheer-on their children or hold their children accountable. What I am saying is, avoid going to extremes, although I also understand that, if you're one of the parents I am talking about, your idea of "extreme" is probably different from mine. Your scale probably differs greatly from the typical college coach, and I understand that too, but don't say you weren't aware. Now you know. We get it, you invest a lot of your time and effort into this but understand that if the things you're communicating to your child affect team chemistry, you're going to be seen as a red flag. If a coach suspects that you might make it difficult to coach your child by expressing your opinions from the sideline, you could easily hurt your child's chances of being recruited.

Coach Harasser

This is the worst. Why? Because this type of parent doesn't understand that a coach has one goal in mind on the court: winning. If you're that parent who texts the coach your ideas after every game, tweets insults about how the game is coached, or constantly shares your unsolicited thoughts about how your kid should be scoring more, stop. You need to understand that no coach is trying to lose. Methods may differ, and mistakes can be made, but when your child plays for the team they're playing for, you're implicitly trusting the coach to make the best decisions for every member of the team, including your child. You're trusting that coach, team, and organization to coach your child. So, Mom, Dad, unless your child is actually being abused, let the coach do their job and have a productive coaching relationship with your child. They need to have open, honest communication with your child to get the best out of them. If you find that you're so unhappy that you find yourself overstepping, maybe you've chosen the wrong coach or program. Trust the coach!

Only you can decide which scenario best fits you and your child, but understand that coaches talk. College coaches are asking your child's HS coach, AAU coach, old AAU coach, old HS coach, etc., and you can be sure they're asking, "How are her parents?" "Will her parents be a problem?" Your reputation matters, and that includes what you post on social media, particularly as it relates to your child's basketball endeavors. Moderation is key. Is it normal to have conversations with your child's coach about their development, performance, etc.? Yes, of course, but there needs to be balance. I'm not a parent, and I would never presume to tell anyone how to raise their child. I have one job here, and that's to inform you how things can be perceived in the recruiting process. Do with it what you desire, and remember, everyone is not for you, nor are you for everyone; and that is okay.

4
How Do I Get Noticed?

Some players are fortunate to have the buzz surrounding them. They've been tweeted about since birth. Others have a little work to do to get noticed. That's the reality of it, and that is OK.

How do I get my daughter looked at? How do we generate more interest? As a college coach, I get these questions all the time, and there's no right or wrong answer. There are many different ways. My opinion on this topic may work for you, and it may not. Some may agree with me, though others may not. The question is usually not asked by the PSAs with 40 offers and who are listed in the top 50. It's usually the PSAs who are at the level where they blend in or they are simply under the radar. These PSA's, who could be you, need to identify ways to separate themselves from the pack, and get a staff's attention. Let's talk about it!

Have A Recruiting Package

In my opinion, the best thing you can do is have your total recruiting package ready. College coaches get hundreds of emails of video highlights and links to recruiting profiles, and so you need to stand out somehow. Each coach is different regarding what they're likely to notice in a positive way. For example, for me, text messages stand out more than emails. Text messages that include the entire package stand out above those that do not, and a text (or email) from a familiar name stands out even more. Let's take a look at how it all works.

Transcripts and Test Scores

Do not underestimate the power of a professional-looking package. Your package should contain your most recent transcripts and SAT or ACT scores, a highlights film, and at least one or, even better, two full-game films. Your test scores and transcripts should be in the most official format possible. Don't submit a picture of your computer screen or a screenshot of your phone. Typically, an acceptable transcript (official or unofficial) will be a document that includes your full name, school name, etc. Scan it and store it as a PDF or, better, download it from your portal as a PDF. The better it looks, the better you're going to look. SAT and ACT sites both allow you to download your full test results in a pdf format as well. Some schools may need to see the full breakdown in writing, reading and math, others may not, but safest to cover all basis.

Highlight and Game Film

Your highlight film is a compilation of plays that show you at your best. It needs to be an attention grabber within the first 30 seconds. I think of highlight films as the appetizer. If coaches watch your highlights and see good things, it's going to whet their appetite to see more. They'll want to see how the strengths that stand out in your highlights film fit into the flow of the game. What they don't want to see is slow-motion clips of you shooting free throws or doing a basic crossover. Just like everything else in this world, if it sparks interest, they're going to look deeper.

Let's talk about game film. Game film is tricky. You're probably looking for your best performance game film to send out, but there are other factors to consider, too, like competition. Who was the game against? Can a coach assess your talent based on who you're playing? What about video quality? Can the coach see your jersey number clearly and identify you? Hopefully you have some decent-quality video of you playing against decent-quality competition. This makes evaluating you straightforward. Many coaches will also want to see you in a bad game. They definitely want to see you at your best, but they also want to see how you perform when the chips are down.

Create a Realistic Target List

You're not blind, and neither are your parents, club coaches, and high school coaches. Your mom and dad may be biased because their little girl has worked so hard. However, you need people who are not going to sugar coat things. Seek out people you trust and will give you honest feedback about your talent. You need an honest assessment as to where your skill level may be the best fit.

In addition to evaluating what level your talent is best suited for, you need to consider what you want from your college experience when you're making your list. Do you want to be an immediate impact player as a freshman? If so, at what schools do you think you can achieve this goal? Do you want to go to a winning program with a history and culture of success? That list of schools may or may not be different. I don't know your talent level, so that is up to you and your circle to decide. There's a variety of questions you can ask yourself to formulate this list, but you should understand and be realistic about what situations can be good for you based on your talent, and the status of each of the current programs. Find realistic situations that you're interested in and create a list of those universities.

I don't think it's ever too soon to start this list for a high school student athlete. Ninth grade is great. Twelfth grade may be late, but opportunities are still out there. Don't be discouraged if you get a late start; just be super intentional and targeted and be good enough for the level you're targeting. That's the whole point. Don't overlook the level of school that's recruiting you. While I'm on this topic, I also want to say this: If you're being recruited by 10 division 2 programs and zero BCS programs, take notice, and use the data to reach informed conclusions. Don't ignore the schools that want you.

RECRUIT THE TARGET

If you're participating in this exercise, it's because you don't feel there's enough recruitment coming your way. Take your future into your own hands. Be a self-starter. Initiate. Own your destiny. Recruit the school. There is zero shame in this method. At the end of it all, the hope is that you end up at an institution that is a good fit for you. How you get there, matters very little. Try this!

1. MAKE DIRECT CONTACT WITH THE STAFF.
Emails are often overlooked. It's a simple fact. Understand that coaches get hundreds of emails per year with film links, bios, etc., and if your name doesn't ring a bell, you could easily be overlooked. This is not to say that a coach will never get around to checking and responding to that email. Most coaches will have splurge moments where they go through and review the many emails received. Because of the extreme overhaul of emails, in my opinion, a phone call alerting the staff that you are sending an email is a great touch. Show your interest in the program, let them know that you would like them to review your film. Once you've made direct contact, your future emails will likely get more immediate notice.

2. RECRUIT THE PROGRAM'S CIRCLE:
Is there anyone you know who has a direct relationship with the staff or program? Not the person who just says, "yes, I know them," but the one who actually knows them. This can be an AAU coach, a trainer, an alum, etc. It's important that you don't have your people making contact on your behalf for situations that are not feasible. I would also think

that whomever you're asking to reach out would have a pulse on this as well. Have that trusted person reach out and communicate your interest. You want this person to be someone who can vouch for your talent and your ability to help the program you've asked them to communicate with. If it comes from a trusted source, college coaches are more likely to take a closer look at you. Now pay close attention here: when those college coaches show up at a game in July, do the work.

COVID: Live evaluations are currently not happening, and this is where your packet comes in handy. And coaches are more likely to look at your package when they've been alerted by a trusted source.

3. ATTEND CAMPS, AND SCHEDULE UNOFFICIAL VISITS:
Once you've established your presence, be visible. Make the effort to attend camps and attend their games. This is easier to do with local institutions. When coaches know who you are or have the ability to work with you in person (in a camp), you're in a stronger position to make a lasting impression. Elite camps can help if you put in work. I've been at institutions where we've extended offers to players, or added players to our board, as a direct result of camp.

COVID: As of this writing, in 2020, COVID-19 precautions have severely curtailed campus visits and camps for obvious reasons. Phone calls, texts, and emails are your best mode of contact under these conditions. Again, this is why your package is so important.

4. FOLLOW UP:
Be persistent, but don't harass them. After you've attended a camp or gotten a staff member to come out and see you, ask for an evaluation. Ask if they see an opportunity for you. If you have an AAU or high school coach who can reach out, they can do it as well. Get feedback! Then you'll know if you're wasting your time. This

can also help you define the group of schools you should be reaching out to. If the program expresses interest, continue to send progress updates throughout your high school season. Continue to build an organic relationship with staffs. You'll notice whether the attention and energy are reciprocated or not. Worst case, you build a relationship that may not be fruitful now, but it might be beneficial down the road.

COVID: Once you know a school has some interest, and has not given an immediate no, work with the staffs to set up Zoom calls. FaceTime with coaches you're talking to. Seeing a person's face is more intimate than phone calls and texts. You may have the ability to make a stronger impression this way.

To reiterate, I've been part of programs (Division 1) that have made offers based on camp attendance and performance. I've been part of programs that have provided walk-on spots based on unofficial visits and have offered opportunities with the added vouching of character and work ethic by a trusted source. Relationships are important in recruiting. If you take nothing else from this book, remember, relationships matter.

Don't be discouraged. Remember, of all the scholarship offers in the world, you can only take one. It may take a little more effort on your part, and that's OK.

5
RESPECT THE PROCESS

Recruitment is a process. Be thankful and appreciative that you're able to go through the process. Not everyone gets the opportunity.

Recruiting is a once-in-a-lifetime opportunity. For college coaches, it's a job, and at the end of the day, we're talking hundreds of thousands of dollars being extended to you. Respect this honor. Communicate in a mature and respectful fashion. Regardless of what recruiting technique coaches use, they're not your friends, and they're not your peers. In the real world, if someone gives you a call, you call them back. If someone sends you a text, you text them back. Given the hundreds of thousands of student athletes a coach could contact, be humble in the fact that they're contacting you. I don't care how good you are or how many offers you have, respect the process. Respect people. It says more about you than you know. You might say, "well, what if I'm not interested in that school?" Keep reading, kid.

NARROW YOUR FOCUS

When you're younger, particularly prior to September 1 of your junior year in high school, colleges may have limited contact with you. In fact, only contact that you initiate is permitted. Colleges may only send you a general questionnaire and camp information prior to September 1 of your junior year, but they cannot initiate anything beyond that. You can call them whenever you like. You can visit them on their campus, provided it falls within legal dates on the recruiting calendar. You essentially control who you have contact with during this phase of recruiting. Many may have conflicting views on how to manage the process at this stage. What I advise is to respect the process whatever way works best for you. The biggest part of respect is communication. If you don't want to communicate with coaches until September 1, communicate that in some way. No one will be upset. Coaches want to know what's going on.

Whether you have 50 schools recruiting you or 2, respect coaches' time and effort. I don't mean that you should worry about how long you carry on conversations; talk as long as you need to get to know the coaches recruiting you—if you're actually interested in the school. When I say respect coaches' time, I mean be honest and transparent. If a college or university from New York contacts you, and you know for a fact that you don't want to go to school on the east coast, tell them! Once you identify the things about a college or university you don't want, inform those coaches so they don't waste their time on you. Inform those coaches so that you don't waste time on them. Don't take up time and effort that they could put toward another potential student athlete who may actually have interest in that school. Don't take time away from homework, gym time, etc. Don't waste people's time.

On the other hand, if this New York school is the only one recruiting you, I would advise you to find some interest and give the process an opportunity, unless you have a better idea. Understand that the more interest you have, the more liberty you'll have in this area. If you have one offer, and that offer is in New York, this is not the time to tell the school in New York you're not interested, unless you'd rather turn down a scholarship and gamble that more will come, or you simply decide not to play college ball. It's totally your choice. There's a very real possibility for whatever you put your mind to. There's no right or wrong; it's all about what's best for you. You just need to be informed when making these decisions. What you may find is that you'll warm up to a school that shows sincere interest in you. There's value in that one school that believes in you when no one else does, so don't ignore that. I've said it before, and I stand firm on this philosophy: go where you are wanted.

BE REALISTIC

Disclaimer: I don't want to hurt any feelings on this one, but there are some harsh truths you may need to hear. If your dream school is the returning national champion that signs top-ten players every year, amazing! Go to their camp, be in the atmosphere, meet the coaches, etc. On the other hand, if, out of the ten offers you have, nine are division 2, chances are that you're a division 2 basketball player, and in most cases, you're probably going to be more successful on the court at that level. Give the schools that want you the love and attention they may deserve in the recruiting process. I'm sorry, but you cannot tell those schools you're not interested because you're waiting for the returning national champs to call you. That's not a smart move. They haven't called yet, and chances are, they will not be calling.

Division 2 basketball is not a bad thing. Let's respect each level for what it is. They all have their perks. Different divisions are better fits for certain people. This would be the same for mid-major, so if, of the 10 offers you have, 9 are low mid-major and one is "BCS," chances are ... well, you know the rest; you may be a mid-major player. It's not a bad thing! I wouldn't dare steer you away from taking that one BCS offer. Just be sure you understand what that BCS program sees in you and how they see you fitting in. Be clear about how they see you and how that aligns with your priorities. It's totally up to you to decide if you want to bet on yourself and go make some splash. Just be ready to do the work. There's really good basketball at all levels, and to play at the collegiate level anywhere is a challenge and a big deal. Remember that.

Take another example: The kid with ten mid-major offers gets a BCS offer late. I see this all the time, and I'm not judging what decision you should make based on this. I just want you to be informed of some situations that can happen behind the scenes in a scenario like this. Perhaps you blew up. You worked your butt off and you had some really good showings as of late. Here come the bigger programs. Perhaps the school lost their first or second options, and guess who's up next? You! You can be excited about this; you can wear a chip on your shoulder about it—you can do whatever you want with it. Just understand, a situation like this could very well mean that you were not the first choice. Who knows where you were on their board? Are you just a body they need to fill a spot? Ask! You want to be very clear about where you stand and what they think of you. How they see you initially may or may not give you the insight you need.

Once you pick a school, how or why you got there has nothing to do with what you do while you're there. Be prepared to do the work. You can work your way into spots even the staff didn't expect you to be in. My entire point in this segment: don't big-time people, especially when the schools you are big-timing are not after you. Take note of the general level of the institutions that are looking at you. This may simply be your level. It's not an absolute, but it's a good rule of thumb.

Go On Unofficial Visits

Regardless of how many offers you have; unofficial visits are a good thing. I know, Mom and Dad may not have the money to fly you around the country and visit every school you want to visit, but at the very least, take unofficial visits to local schools that have expressed interest in you or that you have interest in. While this entire process is about finding what's right for you, there's also value in finding what's not for you. You won't know these things unless you expose yourself to different situations. Do you like private schools or public schools? Big campuses or small ones? Urban or suburban? You won't know until you go and see for yourself. Vibes are real, people interactions are real, face-to-face communication is real, and energy is real. The only way you can get a real feel for a staff or a campus is to go. So, go! As of now, NCAA rules permit you to begin taking official visits upon the completion of the NCAA Final Four tournament of your junior year. Until then, unofficial visits are unlimited and permitted, as long as they fall within the guidelines of the NCAA recruiting calendar. NCAA Recruiting Calendar: The NCAA recruiting calendar can be found at NCAA.org. The calendar will have dead periods and evaluation periods, when unofficial visits are not permitted. This doesn't mean you can't visit the campus, just that the staff cannot have any involvement with the visit. When you communicate with coaching staffs while scheduling these visits, they should have a working knowledge of the dates as well.

NARROW YOUR FOCUS

Going on unofficial visits can also help you narrow your focus. This is especially important, as mentioned earlier. Currently, the NCAA only permits you to make five official visits. If you have more than five scholarship offers, then you obviously cannot make official visits to all of them. Making unofficial visits and being on college campuses can help you decide what feel you want and do not want. For instance, you can take a visit to a private institution and like the feel of a more intimate campus. Conversely, you may also visit a large public school and be overwhelmed. You could walk away saying, "I like a small campus feel," or "I love a big campus feel." These things matter, so be very clear about them. I'm not suggesting that unofficial visits take place of official visits for your local schools should they end up in your top five. Local or not, if they're in your top five, that school deserves a fair shot at giving you the official visit experience, which is very different from the unofficial experience. When you complete your visits and begin your decision-making process, you want to be able to compare apples to apples. Not allowing that school to have an official visit subconsciously puts them at an unfair disadvantage. Use unofficial visits to learn what you like and don't like.

> *COVID:* With unofficial visits not being an option, the internet and relationships are your friend. Talk to people you know and trust, research the programs social media, rosters etc.

RELATIONSHIP BUILDING

Unofficial visits help dramatically with relationships. If there's a local school within driving distance that's highly interested in you and you have an interest in them, visiting with them in person as much as you want has a big upside. You may also take unofficial visits if you are traveling, taking vacations, etc. Anytime you're in the area of a school you've had communication with and are interested in, stop by. Again, you must operate within the NCAA recruiting calendar to make these visits, but unofficial visits are unlimited. Be present, and take some initiative in getting to know the program, the players, the coaches, etc. Coaches do notice and appreciate PSAs who show interest in their programs and recruiting efforts. Think of it as dating: you like it when you're not the only one showing that you're invested.

> ***COVID:*** By now, most college basketball staffs have designed some sort of virtual tour. Be proactive in asking for these things if they have not already been presented to you.

COMMUNICATE

I may sound like a college coach on this point, but I would wager that your club coaches and anyone else affiliated with the game would echo this point: communicate. PSAs underestimate the value of one phone call. There are plenty of other student athletes that a coach could be calling, but they're calling you. Make use of the methods mentioned throughout this book in defining what relationships you want to develop. Whatever you decide, communicate that. Don't have interest in a school? Tell them! Is the process overwhelming for you, and so you only want to take calls on weekends? Tell them! Don't take a single phone call for granted. Each call is a potential opportunity, an opportunity for hundreds of thousands of dollars and to live out your dreams. Your being invested in the process matters.

> "NEVER BURN BRIDGES, YOU AVOID THAT WITH HONESTY AND COMMUNICATION."

While this read will hopefully keep you out of the portal, don't be that kid in the portal reaching out to a school that you treated disrespectfully in the process. Never burn bridges. You can accomplish this with honesty and communication. That same coach you ignored at one school may end up at the school that you want to transfer to somewhere down the line. Don't treat people according to their logo. Relationships matter, so treat each one with care and respect. Coaches may not love hearing that you aren't interested or that you're going elsewhere, but I promise you that every coach prefers to know the truth when you know it. Time is of the essence.

6
THE DECISION

Your fit should be tailored to the things that are important to you. Be intentional in your evaluation process.

This is the exciting part! When I started this book, I wanted to keep it short, and you are now in the home stretch. If it's time to make a decision, you're probably torn and perhaps a little stressed. I personally have always loved making decisions with my gut and intuition, but I also believe that it's important to look at the facts. As long as you're aware of the facts, how you make your final decision is up to you.

Finding your fit should be an individualized process. Your best friend on your club team should not determine your fit. The schools you see everyone else signing to should not determine your fit. Your fit should not be the popular decision. Your decision should be made from among the schools that have actually extended offers to you, or a situation that's feasible, i.e., a walk-on situation. Please note that the dream school that you've had no communication or contact with should not be in this decision-making process. This is for when it's down to the real decision.

You're taking official visits and preparing to commit to just one school. Let's dive in!

What's Important To You?
Determine your non-negotiables

I absolutely adore the "non-negotiables" tag, and as a coach I use it often. It's important to know and understand the things you will not accept under any circumstances. When I say non-negotiables as it relates to finding your fit, I mean, what are the things you know you don't want? Do you know that you don't want to go farther than driving distance from home? Do you know that you don't want to play for a coach with a particular coaching style? Do you know that you need a coach who will push you? Do you know you want to attend a strong academic institution? Do you know you want to be an impact player immediately? The list goes on, and the bottom line is, what do you feel so strongly about that you're not willing to give up?

Be thoughtful about what you designate as non-negotiables. Don't list preferences. Preferences are different from non-negotiables. Preferences are things that you would prefer but could give up under particular circumstances. Keep your list of non-negotiables brief. For example, in my own process, strong academics was a non-negotiable. It didn't have to be top-of-the-line, but I needed it to be a respectable degree. Playing a high level of basketball was a non-negotiable. Having the potential to take a program to new heights was a non-negotiable. Those were my three non-negotiables. There was one item that, in retrospect, probably should've been on my list, but was not, and yes, I ended up in my day's version of the portal: getting a release. Take the time to complete activity 6.1 to come to grips with your non-negotiables, then complete

Activity 6.1

NON-NEGOTIABLES | Be sure to list your non-negotiables in order, beginning with the most important:

> **WHAT ARE THE THINGS YOU KNOW FOR SURE YOU WANT OR DO NOT WANT THAT YOU ARE NOT WILLING TO SACRIFICE? THESE ITEMS WILL BE YOUR "NON-NEGOTIABLES."**
>
> EX. Location — I definitely want to be in state
>
> 1. _____
> 2. _____
> 3. _____
> 4. _____
> 5. _____
> 6. _____
> 7. _____
> 8. _____
> 9. _____
> 10. _____

ACTIVITY 6.2

OFFERS | List all of the schools you will be making your final decision from. Remember, these are only schools you have offers or situations set up with. This is not a list of all schools recruiting you.

> EX 1. South Central Louisiana State University — Partial Scholarship
> EX 2. Faber University — Full Scholarship + in-state grant
> 1. _____
> 2. _____
> 3. _____
> 4. _____
> 5. _____
> 6. _____
> 7. _____
> 8. _____
> 9. _____
> 10. _____

ELIMINATION

Elimination is the tough part. You probably have really good relationships with every school on your final list. The relationships may all feel different, but there's a reason each one is on your list. During the elimination process, don't worry about hurting anyone's feelings. You're the only person who has to live with your decision.

Now that you know your non-negotiables and you've identified your final schools, let's start cutting the list down. Revisit activity 6.2

and cross out any schools that don't align with your non-negotiables. Regardless of how much you like the coach or any other aspect, if you're positive on the things you want and don't want, eliminate. It may be hard, and it may hurt the coach(es), but it's the right thing to do. Eliminate!

Let's say your non-negotiables include strong academics. Take that one school with the not so great academics and the coach you love—sorry, but that school has to go. Regardless of how much you love those people, when you build true relationships, which is what you want to do in this recruiting game, they'll understand when you share what's important to you and when you make decisions based on those factors. Don't be the kid who says you're cutting a school because you want to go to a high-academics institution and then have a low-academics school on your list. At this point, you're not being true to your non-negotiables, and while you have no obligation to share or explain your decisions, just know that you're not in alignment with your own non-negotiables. That, too, is OK. If, after you've laid out your non-negotiables, for some reason your gut is telling you to go to a school that doesn't meet your criteria and that's what you want to do, you need to do some hard thinking. But after you finish this book, you will be informed when making that decision. I just want you to understand and evaluate your choices effectively. The decision you make, and why, is up to you.

Now that you've crossed out the schools that don't align with your non-negotiables, list the schools that remain in the first column of activity 6.3. Hopefully you have enough space for all of your schools. If you have a school that should be eliminated, but you want to keep it along for the ride, go ahead and include that school as well. Just make note of which non-negotiable(s) that school violates. Once you've listed each school, complete the pros and cons columns. Don't answer the yes or no question yet. Just go through and complete the pros and cons. Once you've done so for each school, go back through your list and answer the final column. Do the pros outweigh the cons?

ACTIVITY 6.3

PROS & CONS | List all of the schools you will be making your final decision from. Remember, these are only schools you have offers or situations set up with. This is not a list of all schools recruiting you.

SCHOOL	PROS What are the things you like about this option?	CONS What are the things that you do not like about this option	Do the pros outweigh the cons? (yes/no)
South Central Louisiana State University	1. close to Home 2. love the Coaching Staff 3. likely play right away 4. awesome campus life 5. housing - apartments	1. 1st year no car on campus 2. exact major not avail. 3. weak conference 4. have losing tradition 5. too close to home ???	No
	1. 2. 3. 4. 5. 6. 7. 8. 9. 10.	1. 2. 3. 4. 5. 6. 7. 8. 9. 10.	
	1. 2. 3. 4. 5. 6. 7. 8. 9. 10.	1. 2. 3. 4. 5. 6. 7. 8. 9. 10.	

SCHOOL	PROS What are the things you like about this option?	CONS What are the things that you do not like about this option	Do the pros outweigh the cons? (yes/no)
	1. 2. 3. 4. 5. 6. 7. 8. 9. 10.	1. 2. 3. 4. 5. 6. 7. 8. 9. 10.	
	1. 2. 3. 4. 5. 6. 7. 8. 9. 10.	1. 2. 3. 4. 5. 6. 7. 8. 9. 10.	

Notes: _____

_____

_____

_____

SCHOOL	PROS What are the things you like about this option?	CONS What are the things that you do not like about this option	Do the pros outweigh the cons? (yes/no)
	1. 2. 3. 4. 5. 6. 7. 8. 9. 10.	1. 2. 3. 4. 5. 6. 7. 8. 9. 10.	
	1. 2. 3. 4. 5. 6. 7. 8. 9. 10.	1. 2. 3. 4. 5. 6. 7. 8. 9. 10.	

Notes:
_____
_____
_____
_____

Six Steps To Navigating Your Recruiting Process

SCHOOL	PROS What are the things you like about this option?	CONS What are the things that you do not like about this option	Do the pros outweigh the cons? (yes/no)
	1. 2. 3. 4. 5. 6. 7. 8. 9. 10.	1. 2. 3. 4. 5. 6. 7. 8. 9. 10.	
	1. 2. 3. 4. 5. 6. 7. 8. 9. 10.	1. 2. 3. 4. 5. 6. 7. 8. 9. 10.	

Notes: _____
_____
_____
_____

At this point you should have activity 6.3 completed. Do you still have any schools listed for which the pros do not outweigh the cons? In my opinion they need to go. Here's an example: Let's say that the pros don't outweigh the cons with University of Me. Remember that list of non-negotiables you compiled, starting with most important? What if the University of Me is top of the line in your number one non-negotiable? It gets tricky! That's the reason for this exercise. Perhaps, for you, they stay on the list because that non-negotiable with University of Me is top of the line. I have a high degree of confidence that some other school or schools on your list, the pros of which do outweigh the cons, fulfills that exact same non-negotiable; otherwise they wouldn't be on your list. Do you see where I'm going with this? Why would you choose a school where the pros do not outweigh the cons just to hold on to a superb non-negotiable when the others fulfill the non-negotiable, just not quite at the same level as University of Me? On paper, it doesn't make sense. You can obviously decide to keep this school, but again, the point of this all is that you're aware. You're informed. I want you to understand how each school fits your priorities.

Now that you have information broken down before you to assess, the next thing we're going to do is start comparing final choices. Please complete activity 6.4. Hopefully you've already eliminated some schools by now, but we'll continue with whatever number you have.

ACTIVITY 6.4
Revisit Your Non-Negotiables

STEP 1: For the first part of this activity you'll want to revisit your non-negotiables list in activity 6.1. Again, you'll want to list those items, beginning with most important. It's very important that you do so.

STEP 2: No matter how many non-negotiable items you have, you'll want to number out the "point value" column, beginning with the highest number. For example, if you have six non-negotiables, the first row will be x6. Moving down, it would continue with x5, x4, x3, x2, and end with x1.

ACTIVITY 6.4
EVALUATION | Revisit your non-negotiables:

NON-NEGOTIABLE ITEM	MULTIPLY BY
ex. Location — I definitely want to be in state	x6
1.	
2.	
3.	
4.	
5.	
6.	
7.	
8.	
9.	
10.	

Now we're going to do a little math. The figure will give you an idea of how much each of the schools are in line with your non-negotiables, your priorities, and your fit. List each of your final schools below in the first column. Next, evaluate on a scale from 1-10, 10 being amazing, and you couldn't ask for anything more. For me, University of Me is a 10 in my first non-negotiable. I've listed "close to home" as the most important non-negotiable, so we're going to multiply that by 6 to get 60. Continuing down the list, we will evaluate our second school with respect to "close to home." You want to make sure you evaluate every school on one non-negotiable prior to moving on to the next one. This way, you're using the same scale for that particular item. Let's say the next university scores a 4 on close to home. Multiplying 4 x 6 gives us 24, and so on.

>*STEP 3:* Evaluate your first school with regard to your first non-negotiable. Multiply that rank by the multiple as it corresponds to the image above (column reads "multiply by"). Repeat this process for each school on your list before moving on to a new non-negotiable category.
>
>*STEP 4:* Repeat step 3 for each of your non-negotiable categories. Be sure to complete your evaluations of all schools for one non-negotiable item at a time.
>
>*STEP 5:* Add up the totals for each school and write them in the point total column.
>
>*STEP 6:* In the position rank column, rank your schools from first to last, first being the school with the highest point total. Write the school ranks in the "position rank" column.

ACTIVITY 6.5

COMPARING YOUR FINAL CHOICES | Place all of your options in the chart and compare each using the position rank and point total:

SCHOOL	POINT TALLY BOX	POINT TOTAL	POSITION RANK
Faber University	60 + ? + ? + ? etc...	250	3

Well done! You've finished your math homework for the day. So why did we do all that? What do the numbers show? The school with the highest number is where you should go, right? Wrong! I'm not saying it is the right school and I am not saying it isn't. What you've done is taken the time to evaluate each school as to the things that are truly important to you, the things that make a school your best fit. Regardless of what conclusion you come to, you've done the work and vetted each school through a logical evaluation process, using things that you identified as important.

I want you to review the work you've done in this chapter, starting with the pros and cons list, all the way up to the position ranks you just calculated. Sit with it. Ponder it. Feel it. Understand it. Discuss it. I'm not saying, "that's the school!" That's not what this book is about. You're more informed about your choices and how they align with you. My heart is full.

My Unsolicited Two Cents

While we're on the topic of decisions, it's apparently a thing these days to take five official visits. In my opinion, you don't need five. Truth be told, official visits are exhausting. Ask your college friends who took five. However, the NCAA allows it, and if you think you need all five, by all means do all five. Here's when you shouldn't: If you know for sure that you aren't going to a particular school, save yourself missing a Friday or Monday of school; save your parents missing work and finding babysitters for your siblings; and save the University the money, energy, and stress. This goes back to respecting the process. Don't go on official visits as a vacation. It's silly. Would you want someone to go on a date with you simply because you asked, even though they know they have zero interest in you?

Thank you for having a serious enough interest in your process to open this book. Your reading the book tells me that you want to get it right. You want to find your best fit school and program, and I hope you do. I really do. This text was written for you, along with those in your tribe who will help you through the process. I hope you didn't agree with everything

I wrote. I didn't write it to be right; I wrote it to stimulate thought, to help you with the process, and to give you some insight from a college coach's perspective. These are the things I would tell my little sister, my cousin, or my friend. I wrote the book from my heart, and I thank you for allowing me to share it with you. Take away what resonates and disregard the rest. This process is about what you think and feel. I just hope I helped make my thoughts and feelings clear. As I like to say, Legacy over me! Peace out!

A LETTER FROM THE AUTHOR
2020: COVID-19 and Social Unrest

A note from the Author,

I would be remiss not to take the opportunity to address 2020. I am right there with you. This year has been hard. Mental health and wellness are above all during these times. I hope that you find the time to take care of you regardless of the pressures, and disappointments around you.

One thing you can surely have faith in, is that things will get better.

Continue to stand tall, speak your truth and be unapologetically you.

Tools & Resources

WEBSITES:

NCAA Clearinghouse
https://web3.ncaa.org/ecwr3/

NCAA
http://www.ncaa.org/

Questions To Ask College Coaches

1. How do you see me fitting in on the floor? What do you think are the strengths and weaknesses of my game?

2. How many scholarships do you have available in my class? (Or How many do you plan on signing in my class?)

3. What does a full scholarship consist of? What is your cost of attendance? How do meal plans work as for freshmen and upperclassmen?

4. How do you manage conflicts with class times and practice?

5. How many years do you have on your contract? (intrusive, yes, but necessary)

6. What is your timeline? (you'll want to know how much time you have to decide)

7. How many student athletes have you had transfer out over the past four years?

About Hoop Haus

HOOP HÄUS was founded in 2015 by April Phillips. The brand represents athletes who live a lifestyle that's informed by their love of the game of basketball. The HOOP HÄUS athlete is a monster on the court, not through talent alone, but through a mixture of talent and an extreme work ethic. We hold the game of basketball as a place/state of comfort, a place to call home. We are ambassadors to the athletes who understand that basketball is a means to become an overall Haus at not only the sport, but in life.

Our staff takes pride in enriching individual lives and the community through the game of basketball. We understand that basketball is an intense lifestyle, and yet it is simply a vehicle to achieving personal growth, as an athlete, as a person, and as a path to happiness. We welcome you to browse our website and view a variety of our highly sought-after specialty Tees, hoodies and apparel.

About The Author

April Phillips was born in Los Angeles in 1987 and grew up as an athlete in two sports: track & field and basketball. Basketball soon emerged as her passion, and her love of the game made it her sport of choice. She spent many hours on the sidelines at her brother's practices, and dribbling and shooting, and she soon began playing in the YMCA boys' league at age 5. She went on to play for numerous organized teams and, in the process, earned basketball's most prestigious title: "gym rat."

High school

April attended Narbonne and Long Beach Poly high schools, graduating from Long Beach Poly in 2005. As a high school athlete, she played with organizations such as OGDL and her most prized program, Cal Sparks, earning accolades such as Nike All American, All City, All State, and USA Hoop Festival, among others. She went on to become one of the top 100 athletes in her class and earned a full scholarship to Georgia Tech.

College

After her freshman year at Georgia Tech, April transferred to Florida A&M University, then, shortly thereafter, to Xavier University in Cincinnati. She became a starter on the top 25 Xavier women's basketball team for

2.5 seasons. In her time at Xavier, April became a three-time Atlantic 10 Champion, making a trip to the NCAA tournament each year. Her senior season included a trip to the Elite 8, where her college basketball career ended with a heartbreaking loss to Stanford University at the buzzer.

Following her graduation from Xavier, April received the Thomas E. Sedler award, which distinguishes the senior class athlete who embodies the characteristics of the ideal Xavier University student athlete, both on and off the court or field. She was also featured on the Wall of Fame in the Cintas Center for being the first ever Xavier athlete to reach the post-season in two sports in the same season (track and field, and basketball), earning A10 Championships in both. She also holds shot put records at LB Poly, Georgia Tech and Xavier.

Professional

In 2010, following her final college season, April had a brief career with New York Liberty, working under Anne Donovan. After that, she had an awesome playing career in Israel, Finland, and Belgium. During her final season in Belgium, she averaged 15 points and 15 rebounds per game. After her retirement from the professional game, she began her collegiate coaching career.

Business/training

In 2010, April co-founded S&A Next Level Basketball, with the goal of training and mentoring youth, and founded The CINTAS Summer League in Cincinnati, the region's first ever NCAA certified women's league. The league achieved great success, while bringing in many local college players seeking to sharpen their skills during the off season.

April has worked as a staff member with basketball programs at Seton Hall University, University of New Haven, and, most recently, Georgia Tech. She served as Associate Head Coach / Recruiting Coordinator at Loyola Marymount University in Los Angeles, as well as Assistant Coach/ Recruiting Coordinator at the University of Arizona, and University of California, Berkeley. April has trained top-level high school athletes. Many of her players have gone on to receive division I and division II scholarships and participated in the CINTAS Summer League.

Made in the USA
Las Vegas, NV
23 December 2022

64014721R00060